SENECA ON HAPPINESS, VIRTUE,
AND PHILOSOPHY AS THE GUIDE TO LIFE
Part One of *Seneca of a Happy Life*
by Roger L'Estrange ✱ Edited and Revised by Keith Seddon

Roger L'Estrange, staunch royalist, author and pamphleteer, one-time inmate of Newgate Prison, one-time exile, one-time Member of Parliament, takes up the teaching of the Roman Stoic philosopher Seneca, rearranging and paraphrasing the original Latin to shape a unique and engaging work of his own.

Stoic philosophy guides us through all hazards, and arms us against all difficulties. Those who develop a good character in accordance with Stoic principles learn to live well and face adversities and setbacks with an unshakable equanimity.

This slim volume is the first of three parts of Roger L'Estrange's *Seneca of a Happy Life*, being itself an extract from a much larger whole, *Seneca's Morals*, first published in 1678.

Keith Seddon is professor of philosophy at Warnborough College Ireland.

Roger L'Estrange's *Seneca of a Happy Life* (an extract from *Seneca's Morals By Way of Abstract: To which is added, A Discourse, under the Title of An After-Thought*), edited and revised by Keith Seddon, in Three Parts:

PART ONE
SENECA ON HAPPINESS, VIRTUE, AND
PHILOSOPHY AS THE GUIDE TO LIFE
[Chapters 1–7]

PART TWO
SENECA ON PROVIDENCE, MODERATION,
AND CONSTANCY OF MIND
[Chapters 8–16]

PART THREE
SENECA ON FRIENDSHIP, DEATH,
AND POVERTY
[Chapters 17–25]

OTHER BOOKS BY KEITH SEDDON:

Epictetus: The Discourses, Handbook and Fragments [forthcoming]
The Stoic Fragments of Epictetus [forthcoming]
An Outline of Cynic Philosophy: Antisthenes of Athens and Diogenes of Sinope in Diogenes Laertius Book Six (with C. D. Yonge)
A Summary of Stoic Philosophy: Zeno of Citium in Diogenes Laertius Book Seven (with C. D. Yonge)
Stoic Serenity: A Practical Course on Finding Inner Peace
Epictetus' Handbook and the Tablet of Cebes: Guides to Stoic Living
Lao Tzu: Tao Te Ching
Learning the Tao: Chuang Tzu as Teacher
Tractatus Philosophicus Tao: A short treatise on the Tao Te Ching of Lao Tzu
Time: A Philosophical Treatment

SENECA

ON HAPPINESS, VIRTUE, AND PHILOSOPHY
AS THE GUIDE TO LIFE

Part One
of
Seneca of a Happy Life

An Extract from
SENECA'S MORALS
by
Roger L'Estrange

Edited and Revised by Keith Seddon

LULU

Seneca of a Happy Life, part of *Seneca's Morals By way of Abstract: To which is added, A Discourse, under the Title of An After-Thought* by Roger L'Estrange, was first published in 1678.

This new edition first published 2009
by Keith Seddon
at Lulu
www.lulu.com

© 2009 Keith Seddon

Typeset in Bembo Book 12/15 pt

All rights reserved. No part of this book may be reprinted or reproduced or utilised in any form or by any electronic, mechanical, or other means, now known or hereafter invented, including photocopying and recording, or in any information storage or retrieval system, without permission in writing from the publisher.

ISBN 978–0–9556844–7–0 (paperback)

Misfortunes cannot be avoided; but they may be sweetened, if not overcome, and our lives may be made happy by philosophy.

CONTENTS

Preface	9
To the Reader	15
An After-Thought	17
1. Of a Happy Life, and wherein it Consists	29
2. Human Happiness is founded upon *Wisdom* and *Virtue*; and first of *Wisdom*	33
3. There can be no Happiness without Virtue	39
4. Philosophy is the Guide of Life	50
5. The Force of Precepts	61
6. No Felicity like Peace of Conscience	71
7. A Good Man can never be Miserable, nor a Wicked Man Happy	77

PREFACE

Roger L'Estrange (1616–1704) died just six days before his eighty-eighth birthday, and in the course of his long life he witnessed some of the most momentous upheavals of the seventeenth century: the English Civil Wars, the Interregnum under the Puritan rule of Oliver Cromwell, the Restoration of Charles II, the Popish Plot, and the Glorious Revolution of 1688 which brought William of Orange to the English throne.*

L'Estrange was an ardent Royalist and, in 1644, for his involvement in an unsuccessful attempt to retake the town of King's Lynn in Norfolk from Parliamentarian forces, he was sentenced to death as a spy. The sentence was never carried out, and after being incarcerated in Newgate Prison in London for four years vainly writing numerous petitions that had failed to secure his release, in 1648 'with the privity of his keeper' he escaped to the Continent. Here he stayed, at a variety of locations in Germany and in Holland, until 1653. In that year, under the provisions of the Act of Indemnity, L'Estrange returned to England where he lived quietly until the months preceding the restoration of Charles II in 1660, during which time he devoted himself to publishing a series of pamphlets

---

* The brief biography offered here draws on the only two book-length studies of Roger L'Estrange that were published in English in the last century: *Sir Roger L'Estrange: A Contribution to the History of the Press in the Seventeenth Century*, by George Kitchin (Kegan Paul, Trench, Trubner & Co., 1913), and *Roger L'Estrange and the Making of Restoration Culture*, edited by Anne Dunan-Page and Beth Lynch (Ashgate, 2008).

supporting the royalist cause – earning for himself a reputation as one of Charles II's most radical apologists.

Three years later in 1663, L'Estrange was appointed Surveyor (and then Licenser) of the Press. In order to prevent the promulgation of dissenting publications, he was empowered to conduct searches and seizures at the premises of printers and booksellers, and to pursue his campaign against non-comformists (he was a fierce opponent of religious toleration) he authored his own pamphlets and oversaw the publication of the government newsbook, *The Intelligencer*. Later, he published another paper, *The Observator*, which he wrote singlehandedly, without interruption, from April 1681 to March 1687. It was during this period, in 1685, that L'Estrange received his knighthood from James II (awarded, at least in part, for his contribution between 1678 and 1681 to the exposure of the Popish Plot to assassinate Charles II as a spurious fabrication on the part of the renegade Anglican clergyman Titus Oates). And from 1685 to 1689 he was Member of Parliament for Winchester.

In addition to his journalistic undertakings, L'Estrange also wrote several books, including translations of a number of Greek and Latin classics, including *Aesop's Fables* (still in print in the twenty-first century in much shortened and abridged editions), Cicero's *De Officiis*, and his paraphrases of several of Seneca the Younger's philosophical works collected under the title *Seneca's Morals*. This last book, comprising paraphrased extracts from *On Benefits*, *On the Happy Life*

PREFACE

(from where this present volume is taken), *On Anger*, *On Clemency* and the *Moral Letters*, was first published in 1678, and its popularity – indeed, it was one of his most popular works* – was such that by the time of L'Estrange's death in 1704, the book had already been issued in its eighth edition. By 1735 it had reached its twelfth edition. Further editions, from both British and American publishes, were issued throughout the nineteenth century.

The text of all three volumes of this current edition of Roger L'Estrange's *Seneca of a Happy Life* is based on the 1702 eighth edition of *Seneca's Morals* printed by W. Bowyer for Jacob Tonson. In revising it, I have referred to a handful of other editions, including the 1739 fourteenth edition, the 1755 sixteenth edition, several from the 19th century, and one from the 20th century. These later editions often make sweeping changes to the punctuation, sometimes confusing or altering the meaning, and occasionally contain errors, including omitted words, and words changed into completely different words. My hope is that in returning to an earlier edition of this work, one that was published in the author's lifetime, and perhaps overseen by the author himself, the present text offered here is as close to the author's meaning as it is possible to approximate.

This present series of volumes constitute the first new publication of Roger L'Estrange's writings for

---

* See Duncan-Page and Lynch op. cit. p. 218.

almost a century,* the last being an edition of *Seneca's Morals* published in 1917 – the 'centennial edition' – which reproduces in typographical facsimile the 1817 fifth American edition published by Evert Duyckinck in New York.

In his note 'To the Reader' at the front of the book, L'Estrange explains that a straightforward translation of Seneca would not be up to the job because it would entail the inclusion of all sorts of material that does not interest him, not to mention the 'frequent repetitions' that he complains of in Seneca's writing.† In addition to which his proposal for his own brief and properly ordered book would be at odds with the source material that lacks 'any regulated method of discourse', consisting rather in 'divine and extraordinary hints and notions'. Instead, he will 'abstract' the material that he considers worthy of proper attention, and present it in a paraphrase, collecting Seneca's 'scattered ethics' under proper headings. L'Estrange expounds at length (in his 'After-Thought', which is included below) on his reasons for treating Seneca as he does.

L'Estrange laments his inability to render Seneca in the spirit of the original prose, and that had he been able to do so, his book would be 'one of the most valuable presents that ever any private man bestowed upon the public'.‡ If the author bemoans the quality of

---

* Except for just one facsimile reprint (published in 2008) of 'A New Edition' printed in London for Sherwood, Neely and Jones in 1818.
† See page 15, below.
‡ Page 16, below.

PREFACE

his own writing, it is his reader's prerogative to judge differently. It was by sheer chance, having already read all the writings of the ancient Stoics in modern translations, that I stumbled upon Roger L'Estrange's book. The first edition I acquired was a worn and battered printing of the sixteenth edition of 1755, its pages stained by use and age, its original leather binding badly scratched and scared, though miraculously still intact. The book gives every appearance that its owners had made sustained practical use of it, carried it in their pockets (for indeed, a book this size was designed with that very purpose in mind), opened it to their favourite passages in their hours of need when other comforts and consolations were lacking. L'Estrange paraphrases Seneca, saying that

> The true felicity of life is to be free from perturbations, to understand our duties toward God and man, and to enjoy the present without any anxious dependence upon the future.*

In showing through his paraphrase how Seneca elucidates what the 'felicity of life' consists in, and how those who are drawn to the Stoic outlook might do away with hopes and fears, stand firm against the whims of fortune, and bear all things with an equanimity of spirit that defies the understanding of almost everyone – showing us these things is what makes L'Estrange's book 'the most valuable present'. For

---

* See page 30, below.

whatever else it may be, Stoic philosophy is a therapy for miseries and misfortunes once they have occurred, and proof against their recurrence in the future – for those folk, at least, who turn to philosophy as the 'art and law of life',* and apply themselves to learning its lessons.

When reading Roger L'Estrange, it is hard to resist the thought that in him, surely, we find a man who understood the source of his troubles (the same source from which spring the troubles of all mankind), and that his taking up Stoic philosophy as a lived experience provided an effective remedy against those troubles. Although we all fall short of attaining the unbreakable peace of mind enjoyed by the Stoic Sage in whom the Stoic outlook is utterly perfected, we can nevertheless hopefully journey alongside Roger L'Estrange and travel to a place that is better than our current lodging.

---

* See page 51, below.

TO THE READER

IT has been a long time in my thought to turn *Seneca* into *English*. But whether as a *translation*, or an *abstract*, was the *question*. A *translation* I perceive it must not be, at last, for several reasons. First, it is a thing already done to my hand, and above sixty years standing; though with as little *credit* perhaps to the *Author*, as *satisfaction* to the *Reader*. Secondly, there is a great deal in him that is wholly foreign to my business: as his philosophical Treatises of *Meteors*, *Earthquakes*, the Original of *Rivers*, several frivolous Disputes betwixt the *Epicureans* and the *Stoics*, &c. to say nothing of the frequent repetitions of the same thing again in other words (wherein he very handsomely excuses himself, by saying *that he does but inculcate over and over the same counsels to those that over and over commit the same faults*). Thirdly, his excellency consists rather in a *rhapsody* of divine and extraordinary *hints* and *notions* than in any regulated *method* of discourse; so that to take him as he lies, and so to go through with him, were utterly inconsistent with the *order* and *brevity* which I propound; my principal design being only to digest and common-place his *Morals*, in such sort, that any man, upon occasion, may know where to find them. And I have kept myself so close to this proposition that I have reduced all his *scattered Ethics* to their *proper heads*, without any additions of my own, more than of absolute necessity for the tacking of them together. Some other man in my place would perhaps make you twenty apologies for his want of skill and address in governing this affair, but these are *formal* and *pedantic fooleries*, as if any man that first takes himself for a coxcomb in his own heart would afterwards make himself one in print too. This *Abstract*, such as it is, you are extremely welcome to; and I am sorry it is no better, both for your sakes and my own: for if it were written up to the spirit of the *original*, it would be one of the most valuable presents that ever any private man bestowed upon the public: and this too, even in the judgement of both parties, as well Christian as Heathen: of which in its due place.

Next to my choice of the *Author*, and of the *subject*, together with the manner of handling it, I have likewise had some regard in this publication to the *timing* of it ... We are fallen into an age of *vain philosophy* (as the holy apostle calls it), and so desperately overrun with *Drolls* and *Sceptics*, that there is hardly anything so certain or so sacred that is not exposed to *question* and *contempt*, insomuch, that betwixt the *hypocrite* and the *Atheist*, the very foundations of *religion* and *good manners* are shaken, and the two tables of the *Decalogue* dashed to pieces the one against the other. The laws of government are subjected to the fancies of the vulgar; public authority to the private passions and opinions of the people; and the supernatural motions of grace confounded with the common dictates of Nature. In this state of corruption, who so fit as a good honest *Christian Pagan* for a moderator among *Pagan-Christians*?

... The reader will, in some measure, be able to judge ... as to the cast of my design and the simplicity

AN AFTER-THOUGHT

of the style and dress.... Whether it pleases the world or no, the care is taken; and yet I could wish that it might be as delightful to others upon the perusal as it has been to me in the speculation. Next to the gospel itself, I do look upon it as the most sovereign remedy against the miseries of human nature; and I have ever found it so, in all the injuries and distresses of an unfortunate life....

AN AFTER-THOUGHT

THIS abstract has now passed the fifth impression, but the world has not been altogether so kind of late to my politics as to my Morals.* And what is the meaning of it, but that we live in an age that will better bear the image of what people ought to do than the history of what they do? And that is the difference they put betwixt the one and the other. We are not yet to take an estimate of the intrinsic value of truth, honesty, and reason, by fancy or imagination; as if the standard of virtue were to be accommodated to the various changes and vicissitudes of times, interests, and contending parties. But so it falls out that some verities and some good offices will take a false colour better than others, and set off an impos-

---

* He means by 'my Morals' his book, *Seneca's Morals*. This 'After-Thought', in keeping with its title, is placed by L'Estrange at the very end of his book. For this edition, it seems appropriate to place it here, because it continues and expands the discussion already started in the note 'To the Reader'.

ture with more credit and countenance to the common people. Daily experience tells us that our affections are as liable to be vitiated as our palates, insomuch that the most profitable of meats, drinks, or remedies, lose not only their effect but their very savor, and give us a loathing at one time for that we longed for and took delight in at another. But then we are to consider that the humour may come about again, and that writings and opinions have their seasons too, and take their turns, as well as all other changeable things under the sun. So that, let error, corruption, or iniquity, be never so strong, never so popular; let the ignorance of things necessary to be known, be never so dark and palpable, we may yet assure ourselves that however truth and justice may suffer a temporary eclipse, they will yet, at the long run, as certainly vindicate themselves and recover their original glory as the setting sun shall rise again.

When I speak of *my Morals,* let me not be understood to play the plagiary, and to assume the subject-matter of this work to myself; for it is *Seneca's*, every thought and line of it: though it would be as hard to refer each sentence, text, and precept, to the very place whence it was drawn, as to bring every distinct drop in a cask of wine to the particular grape from whence it was pressed. So that I have no other claim to the merit of this composition than the putting of things in order that I found in confusion; and digesting the loose minutes, and the broken meditations of that divine Heathen, into a kind of system of good counsels and of good manners. But how faithfully soever I have dealt with my Author, in a just and genuine representation of his sense and meaning, so have I, on the other hand, with no less conscience and affection, consulted the benefit, the ease, and the satisfaction of the English reader in the plainness and simplicity of the style, and in the perspicuity of the method. And yet, after all this, there is somewhat still wanting, methinks, toward the doing of a full right to *Seneca*, to the world, and to myself, and to the thorough-finishing of this piece: a thing that I have had in my head long and often, and which I have as good a will to prosecute, even at this instant, as ever, if I could but flatter myself with day enough before me to go through with it. But before I come to the point under deliberation, it will do well, first to take a view of the true state of the matter in hand, upon what ground we stand at present. Secondly, to consider from whence it is that we are to take our rise to it; and so to open briefly, and by degrees, into the thing itself.

This abstract, I say, is entirely *Seneca's*, and ... it is, in effect, a summary of the whole body of his philosophy concerning manners contracted into this epitome, without either overcharging it with things idle and superfluous, or leaving out anything which I thought might contribute to the order and dignity of the work. As to his school-questions and philosophical disquisitions upon the natural reason of things, I have almost totally cast them out, as curiosities that hold little or no intelligence with the government of our passions and the forming of our lives, and as matters, consequently, that are altogether foreign to my province. I have taken the liberty also, in many cases, where our Author inculcates and enforces the same conceptions over and over again in variety of phrase, to extract the spirit of them; and instead of dressing up the same thought in several shapes, to make some one adequate word or sentence serve for all. But when all is said that can be said, nay, and when all is done too that can be done, within the compass of an essay of this quality; though never so correct in the kind, it is at the best but an abstract still; and a bare abstract will never do the business as it ought to be done.

It is not one jot derogatory to *Seneca's* character to observe upon him, that he made it his profession, rather to give lights and hints to the world, than to write *corpuses* of morality, and prescribe rules and measures in a set course of philosophy for the common instruction of mankind: so that many of his thoughts seem to spring only like sparks, upon a kind of collision, or striking of fire, within himself, and with very little dependence sometimes one upon another. What if those incomparable starts and strictures of his, that no translator can lay hold of, shall be yet allowed by the common voice of mankind, to be as much superior to those parts of him that will bear the turning, as the faculties and operations of the soul are to the functions of the body? And no way of conveying the benignity of those influences to the world but by a speculation upon them in paraphrase. In few words: *Seneca* was a man made for meditation. He was undoubtedly a master of choice thoughts, and he employed the vigour of them upon a most illustrious subject. Beside that, this ranging humour of his (as Mr. Hobbes expresses it) is accompanied with so wonderful a felicity of lively and pertinent reflections, even in the most ordinary occurrences of life, and his applications so happy also, that every man reads him over again within himself, and feels and confesses in his own heart the truth of his doctrine. What can be done more than this now in the whole world toward establishing of a right principle? For there is no test of the truth and reason of things like that which has along with it the assent of Universal Nature. As he was much given to thinking, so he wrote principally for thinking men; the periods that he lays most stress upon are only so many detachments of one select thought from another, and every fresh hint furnishes a new text to work upon. So that the reading of *Seneca* without reading upon him, does but the one half of our business; for his innuendoes are infinitely more instructive than his words at length, and there is no coming at him in those heights without a paraphrase.

It will be here objected that a paraphrase is but the reading upon a text, or an arbitrary descant upon the original, at the will and pleasure of the interpreter. If we have all of *Seneca's* that is good already, there is no place left for a supplement, and the animadversion will be no more *Seneca's* at last than our comments upon the Word of God are holy writ.

A paraphrase, it is true, may be loose, arbitrary, and extravagant. And so may anything else that ever was committed to writing; nay, the best and the most necessary of duties, faculties, and things, may degenerate by the abuse of them, into acts of sin, shame, and folly. Men may blaspheme in their prayers, they may poison one another in their cups or in their porridge. They may talk of treason; and, in short, they may do a million of extravagant things in all cases and offices that any man can imagine under the sun. And what is the objector's inference now, from the possibility of this abuse, but that we are neither to pray, nor to eat, nor to drink, nor to open our mouths, nor in fine, to do anything else for fear of more *possibilities* as dangerous as the other? It is suggested again, that the paraphrase is foreign to the text, and that the animadvertor may make the Author speak what he pleases. Now, the question is not the possibility of a vain, an empty, a flat, or an unedifying exposition; but the need, the use, the means, the possibility, nay, and the easiness of furnishing a good one. Beside that, there is no hurt at all, on the one hand to countervail a very considerable advantage to all men of letters, and of common honesty on the other. A short or an idle comment does only disgrace the writer of it, while the reputation of the Author stands nevertheless as firm as ever it did; but he that finishes *Seneca's* minutes with proper and reasonable supplements, where he does not speak his own thoughts out at large, does a necessary right both to the dead, and to the living, and a common service to mankind.

He does a right to the dead, I say, more ways than one: for over and above the justice and respect that is due to his memory, it is, in a fair equity of construction, a performance of the very will of the dead. For

AN AFTER-THOUGHT

all his fragments of hint, and essay, were manifestly designed for other people to meditate, read, and speculate upon: and a great part of the end of them is lost without such an improvement; so that the very manner of his writings call for a paraphrase; a paraphrase he expected, and a paraphrase is due to him; and, in short, we owe a paraphrase to ourselves too: for the meaning of his hints and minutes does as well deserve to be expounded, as the sense and energy of his words. Nay, and when all is done, whoever considers how he diversifies the same thing over and over in a change of phrase; how many several ways he winds and moulds his own thoughts; and how he labours under the difficulty of clearing even his own meaning – whoever considers this, I say, will find *Seneca*, upon the whole matter, to be in a great measure a paraphrast upon himself. He gives you his first sense of things, and then he enlarges upon it, improves it, distinguishes, expounds, dilates, &c; and when he finds at last that he cannot bring up the force of his words to the purity and vigour of his conception, so as to extricate himself in all respects to his own satisfaction, it is his course commonly to draw the stress of the question to a point, and there to let it rest, as a theme of light that stands effectually recommended to farther consideration. This must not be taken as if *Seneca* could not speak his own mind, as full and as home as any man; or as if he left anything imperfect because he could not finish it himself. But it was a turn of art in him, by breaking off with an &c. to create an *appetite* in the reader of pursuing the hint; over and above the flowing of matter so fast upon him, that it was impossible for his words to keep pace with his thoughts.

Be this now spoken with all reverence to his divine Essays upon Providence, *Happy* Life, Benefits, Anger, Clemency, Human Frailty, &c. where he shows as much of skill in the distribution of his matter, the congruity and proportion of the parts, and the harmony of the whole in the context, as he does of a natural felicity in adapting the tendency and the virtue of all his sententious raptures to the use of human life. So that he was evidently in possession of both faculties (of *springing game,* that is, and of flying it home) though he made choice of exercising the one oftener than the other. There is a vein of this mixture that runs through all his discourses, whether broken or continued. Albeit, that there is no touching any piece of his to advantage after he has finished it: there is room abundantly yet for explication, and for supplement in other cases, where he snaps off short with a kind of *cætera desiderantur,* and so leaves a foundation for those to build upon that shall come after him. Now, these independent thoughts are the touches that I would offer to a farther improvement, and only here and there one of the most elevated even of them too, which will amount to no more in the conclusion than a discourse upon this or that theme or text, under what name or title the expositor pleases. I would not however have the comment break in upon the context; and I would scrupulously confine it to the bounds of modesty and conscience, as not to depart upon any terms, either from the intent of the original, or from the reason of the matter in question. This office performed, would raise another *SENECA* out of the ashes of the former, and make, perhaps, a manual of salutary precepts, for the ordering of our passions and for the regulation of our lives, not inferior to any other whatsoever, the divine oracles of holy inspiration only excepted. For it would reach all states of men, all conditions of fortune, all distresses of body, all perturbations of mind; and, in fine, it would answer all the ends that are worthy of an honest man's care. It was once in my head to digest the whole into such an abstract, as might at the same time do the office also of a paraphrase, both under one; but what with the scruple of either assuming any of *SENECA's* excellencies to myself, or of imputing any of my weaknesses to *SENECA*, I compounded the matter thus within myself, that though both would do well, the doing of them separate and apart would be best. Not but that the undertaker, I fear, will find well-nigh as much difficulty to preserve his own reputation in his attempt, as to do right to the Author, especially when he is sure to have every coffee-house sit upon him like a court of justice, and if he shall but happen to stumble upon any of the same figures or illustrations over again – if the *supplement* shall but have so much as the least tincture of anything that is done already, a common criminal, for the basest sort of washing, clipping, and coining, shall find better quarter. Here is the old abstract, they will cry, juggled into a new paraphrase, and the same thing fobbed upon the world over again, only under another name. It will be hard to get clear of such a cavil when it shall be started, and it will be a very easy thing to find out a plausible colour for the setting of it afoot.

As to the supposal of disparaging an excellent Author by a lewd paraphrase, it is as idle as to imagine that a canonical text should suffer for an heretical interpretation. And so for the fancy of robbing him of his due by a good one, in a case where the single point is only a virtuous emulation betwixt them which shall do best upon the same topic. Now, where the comment has a kindness for the text, there can be no interfering upon a pique of honour, though they should both happen to agree in the very self-same thoughts. For what is all the writing, reading, discoursing, consulting, disputing, meditating, compounding, and dividing, from the first quickening breath of the Almighty into reasonable Nature to this very moment; what is all this, I say, but the lighting of one candle at another? Make it the case that by the benefit of that light I find a treasure. Here is no robbing of *Peter* to pay *Paul*, nor any particular obligation for an act of common humanity. Reason works by communication, and one thought kindles another from generation to generation, as naturally as one spark begets another, where the matter is disposed for the impression.

This is no more than to say that Providence, for the good of mankind, has made all men necessary one to another. He that puts a good hint into my head, puts a good word into my mouth, unless a blockhead has it in keeping: so that there is an obligation on both sides. The text is beholden to him that reads upon it for

AN AFTER-THOUGHT

improving it, and the latter had never thought of the subject perhaps, if the former had not bolted it. What is all this now but reasoning upon first motions, and a joining of those two powers or faculties both in one for a public good? Reason is uniform; and where two men are in the right, they must of necessity agree upon the same point; and the thoughts of several men in such a case are as much one as a conflagration is one fire, by how many several hands soever it was kindled: so that there is no saying which was one's thought or which the other's; but they are incorporated into one common stock. The great nicety will lie in a judicious choice what to take and what to leave; where to begin and where to end; and in hitting the precise medium betwixt too much and too little, without forcing the design of the Author, or intermixing any tawdry flourishes by the by to disgrace the dignity of the matter. I would not have so much as one word inserted that might not become *SENECA* himself if he were now living either to speak or to approve. Once for all, such a reading upon *SENECA* as I have here propounded upon these terms and under these conditions, and in such a manner too, as to take the genuine air and figure of his mind in its native simplicity and beauty – such a paraphrase, I say, superadded by way of supplement where the Abstract falls short, would furnish us with that which of all things in the world we want the most: that is to say, a perfect and a lively image of HUMAN NATURE.

CHAPTER I

OF A HAPPY LIFE, AND WHEREIN IT CONSISTS

THERE is not anything in this world, perhaps, that is more talked of, and less understood, than the business of a *happy life*. It is every man's wish and design, and yet not one of a thousand that knows wherein that happiness consists. We live however in a blind and eager pursuit of it, and the more haste we make in a wrong way, the farther we are from our journey's end. Let us therefore *first* consider, *what it is we would be at* and *secondly, which is the readiest way to compass it*. If we be right, we shall find every day how much we improve; but if we either follow the cry, or the track of people that are out of the way, we must expect to be misled, and to continue our days in wandering and error. Wherefore, it highly concerns us to take along with us a skilful guide; for it is not in this, as in other voyages, where the highway brings us to our place of repose; or, if a man should happen to be out, where the inhabitants might set him right again. But on the contrary, the beaten road is here the most dangerous, and the people, instead of helping us, misguide us. Let us not therefore follow like beasts, but rather govern ourselves by *reason* than by *example*. It fares with us in human life as in a routed army; one stumbles first, and then another falls upon him, and so they follow, one upon the neck of another, until the whole field comes to be but one heap of miscarriages. And the mischief is, *that the number of the multitude carries it against truth and justice*, so that we must leave the crowd if we would be happy. For the question of a *happy life* is not to be decided by *vote*: nay, so far from it that plurality of voices is still an argument of the wrong; the common people find it easier to believe than to judge, and content themselves with what is usual, never examining whether it be good or no. By the *common people* is intended *the man of title* as well as the *clouted shoe*; for I do not distinguish them by the eye, but by the mind, which is the proper judge of the man. Worldly felicity, I know, makes the head giddy, but if ever a man comes to himself again, he will confess that *whatsoever he has done, he wishes undone*, and that *the things he feared were better than those he prayed for*.

True happiness

THE true felicity of *life* is to be free from perturbations, to understand our duties toward God and man, and to enjoy the present without any anxious dependence upon the future. Not to amuse ourselves with either hopes or fears, but to rest satisfied with what we have, which is abundantly sufficient; for he that is so, wants nothing. The great blessings of mankind are within us, and within our reach, but we shut our eyes, and like people in the dark we fall foul upon the very thing we search for, without finding it. *Tranquillity is a certain equality of mind, which no condition of fortune can either exalt or depress.* Nothing can make it less, for it is the state of human perfection. It raises us as high as we can go and makes every man his own supporter; whereas he that is borne up by anything else may fall. He that judges aright, and perseveres in it, enjoys a perpetual calm. He takes a true prospect of things, he observes an order, measure, a *decorum* in all his actions. He has a benevolence in his nature, he squares his life according to reason, and draws to himself love and admiration. Without a certain and an unchangeable judgement, all the rest is but fluctuation. But *he that always wills and wills the same thing, is undoubtedly in the right.* Liberty and serenity of mind must necessarily ensue upon the mastering of those things which either allure or affright us, when, instead of those flashy pleasures (which even at the best are both vain and hurtful together), we shall find ourselves possessed of joys transporting and everlasting. It must be a *sound mind* that makes a *happy man*; there must be a constancy in all conditions, a care for the things of this world, but without trouble, and such an indifference for the bounties of fortune that either with them or without them, we may live contentedly. There must be neither lamentation nor quarrelling, nor sloth, nor fear, for it makes a discord in a man's life. *He that fears, serves.* The joy of a wise man stands firm without interruption. In all places, at all times, and in all conditions, his thoughts are cheerful and quiet. As it never *came in* to him from *without*, so it will never leave him, but it is born within him, and inseparable from him. It is a solicitous life that is egged on with the hope of anything, though never so open and easy, nay, though a man should never suffer any sort of disappointment. I do not speak this either as a bar to the fair enjoyment of lawful pleasures or to the gentle flatteries of reasonable expectations. But on the contrary, I would have men to be always in good humour, provided that it arises from their own souls and be cherished in their own breasts. Other delights are trivial; they may smooth the brow, but they do not fill and affect the heart. *True joy is a serene and sober motion*, and they are miserably out that take *laughing* for *rejoicing*. The seat of it is within, and there is no cheerfulness like the resolution of a brave mind that has fortune under its feet. He that can look death in the face and bid it welcome, open his door to poverty and bridle his appetites, this is the man whom Providence has established in the possession of inviolable delights. The pleasures of the vulgar are ungrounded, thin, and superficial; but the others are solid and *eternal*. As the *body* itself is rather a *necessary thing* than a *great*, so the comforts of it are but temporary and vain; beside that, without extraordinary moderation, their end is only pain and repentance. Whereas a peaceful conscience, honest thoughts, virtuous actions, and an indifference for casual events, are blessings without end, satiety, or measure. This consummated state of felicity is only a submission to the dictate of right Nature, *The foundation of it is wisdom and virtue; the knowledge of what we ought to do, and the conformity of the will to that knowledge.*

CHAPTER 2

HUMAN HAPPINESS IS FOUNDED UPON WISDOM AND VIRTUE; AND FIRST OF WISDOM

TAKING for granted that *human happiness* is founded upon *wisdom* and *virtue*, we shall treat of these two points in order as they lie. And *first* of *wisdom*: not in the latitude of its various operations, but only as it has a regard to good life and the happiness of mankind.

WISDOM is a right understanding, a faculty of discerning good from evil, what is to be chosen and what rejected, a judgment grounded upon the value of things, and not the common opinion of them; an equality of force, and a strength of resolution. It sets a watch over our words and deeds, it takes up with the contemplation of the works of Nature, and makes us invincible, either by good or evil fortune. It is large and spacious, and requires a great deal of room to work in; it ransacks heaven and earth; it has for its object things past and to come, transitory and eternal. It examines all the circumstances of time: *what it is, when it began, and how long it will continue:* and so for the mind, *whence it came, what it is, when it begins, how long it lasts, whether or no it passes from one form to another, or serves only one, and wanders when it leaves us; where it abides in the state of separation, and what the action of it; what use it makes of liberty, whether or no it retains the memory of things past, and comes*

Wisdom, what it is

to the knowledge of itself. It is the habit of a perfect mind and the perfection of humanity raised as high as Nature can carry it. It differs from *philosophy*, as avarice and money; the one desires, and the other is desired; the one is the effect and the reward of the other. To be wise is the use of wisdom, as seeing is the use of eyes, and well speaking the use of eloquence. He that is perfectly wise is perfectly happy; nay, the very beginning of wisdom makes life easy to us. Neither is it enough to know this unless we print it in our minds by daily meditation, and so bring a *good will* to a *good habit*. And we must practise what we preach: for *philosophy* is not a subject for popular ostentation, nor does it rest in words, but in things. It is not an entertainment taken up for delight, or to give a taste to our leisure, but it fashions the mind, governs our actions, tells us what we are to do, and what not. It sits at the helm and guides us through all hazards; nay, we cannot be safe without it, for every hour gives us occasion to make use of it. It informs us in all the duties of life, piety to our parents, faith to our friends, charity to the miserable, judgment in counsel; it gives us *peace* by *fearing* nothing, and *riches* by *coveting nothing*.

THERE is no condition of life that excludes a wise man from discharging his duty. If his fortune be good, he *tempers* it; if bad, he *masters* it; if he has an estate, he will exercise his virtue in plenty; if none, in poverty: if he cannot do it in his country, he will do it in banishment; if he has no command, he will do the office of a common soldier. Some people have the skill of

A wise man does his duty in all conditions

reclaiming the fiercest of beasts: they will make a lion embrace his keeper, a tiger kiss him, and an elephant kneel to him. This is the case of a wise man in the extremest difficulties; let them be never so terrible in themselves, when they come to him once they are perfectly tame. They that ascribe the invention of tillage, architecture, navigation, &c. to wise men may perchance be in the right, that they were invented by wise men; but they were not invented by wise men, as *wise men*, for wisdom does not teach our fingers, but our minds. Fiddling and dancing, arms and fortifications, were the works of luxury and discord; but wisdom instructs us in the way of Nature, and in the arts of unity and concord, not in the instruments, but in the government of life; nor to make us live only, but to live happily. She teaches us what things are good, what evil, and what only appear so, and to distinguish betwixt true greatness and tumour. She clears our minds of dross and vanity. She raises up our thoughts to heaven, and carries them down to hell. She discourses of the nature of the soul, the powers and faculties of it, the first principles of things, the order of providence. She exalts us from things corporeal to incorporeal, and retrieves the truth of all. She searches Nature, gives laws to life, and tells us that *It is not enough to know God, unless we obey him*. She looks upon all accidents as acts of Providence, sets a true value upon things, delivers us from false opinions, and condemns all pleasures that are attended with repentance. She allows nothing to be good that will not be so for ever; no man to be happy but he that needs no other happiness than what he has within himself; no man to be great, or powerful, that is not master of himself. This is the felicity of human life, a felicity that can neither be corrupted nor extinguished. It enquires into the nature of the heavens, the influence of the stars, how far they operate upon our minds and bodies; which thoughts, though they do not form our manners, they do yet raise and dispose us for glorious things.

IT is agreed on all hands that *Right reason is the perfection of human nature*, and wisdom only the dictate of it. The greatness that arises from it is solid and unmoveable, the resolutions of wisdom being free, absolute, and constant; whereas folly is never long pleased with the same thing, but still shifting of counsels and sick of itself. There can be no happiness without constancy and prudence, for a wise man is to write without a blot, and what he likes once he approves forever. He admits of nothing that is either evil or slippery, but marches without staggering or stumbling, and is never surprised. He lives always true and steady to himself, and whatsoever befalls him, this great artificer of both fortunes turns to advantage. He that demurs and hesitates is not yet composed. But wheresoever virtue interposes upon the main, there must be concord and consent in the parts. For all virtues are in agreement, as well as all vices are at variance. A wise man, in what condition soever he is, will be still happy, for he subjects all things to himself, because he submits himself to reason, and governs his actions by counsel, not by

Right reason is the perfection of human nature

passion. He is not moved with the utmost violences of fortune, nor with the extremities of fire and sword; whereas a fool is afraid of his own shadow and surprised at ill accidents, as if they were all levelled at him. He does nothing unwillingly, for whatever he finds necessary, he makes it his choice. He propounds to himself the certain scope and end of human life: he follows that which conduces to it, and avoids that which hinders it. He is content with his lot, whatever it be, without wishing what he has not; though of the two, he had rather abound than want. The great business of his life, like that of Nature, is performed without tumult or noise. He neither fears danger, nor provokes it, but it is his caution, not any want of courage; for captivity, wounds and chains, he only looks upon as false and lymphatical terrors. He does not pretend to go through with whatever he undertakes, but to do that well which he does. Arts are but the servants, wisdom commands; and where the matter fails, it is none of the workman's fault. He is cautious in doubtful cases, in prosperity temperate, and resolute in adversity; still making the best of every condition, and improving all occasions to make them serviceable to his fate. Some accidents there are, which I confess may affect him, but not overthrow him; as bodily pains, loss of children and friends, the ruin and desolation of a man's country. One must be made of stone or iron, not to be sensible of these calamities; and beside, it were no virtue to *bear* them, if a body did not *feel* them.

THERE are *three degrees of proficients* in the school of wisdom. The *first* are those that come within the sight of it, but not up to it. They have learned what they ought to do, but they have not put their knowledge in practice. They are past the hazard of a relapse, but they have still the grudges of a disease, though they are out of the danger of it. By a disease, I do understand an obstinacy in evil or an ill habit that makes us over-eager upon things, which are either not much to be desired, or not at all. A *second* sort are those that have subjected their appetite for a season, but are yet in fear of falling back. A *third* sort are those that are clear of many vices, but not of all. They are not covetous, but perhaps they are choleric; not lustful, but perchance ambitious; they are firm enough in some cases, but weak in others. There are many that despise death, and yet shrink at pain. There are diversities in wise men, but no inequalities; one is more affable, another more ready, a third a better speaker, but the felicity of them all is equal. It is in this, as in heavenly bodies; there is a *certain* state in greatness.

Three degress of proficients in wisdom

IN civil and domestic affairs a wise man may stand in need of counsel, as of a physician, an advocate, a solicitor, but in greater matters, the blessing of wise men rests in the joy they take in the communication of their virtues. If there were nothing else in it, a man would apply himself to wisdom, because it settles him in a perpetual tranquillity of mind.

A wise man in some cases may need counsel

CHAPTER 3

THERE CAN BE NO HAPPINESS WITHOUT VIRTUE

VIRTUE is that perfect good which is the complement of a *happy life*, the only immortal thing that belongs to mortality. It is the knowledge both of others and itself; it is an invincible greatness of mind, not to be elevated or dejected with good or ill fortune. It is sociable and gentle, free, steady and fearless, content within itself, full of inexhaustible delight, and it is valued for itself. One may be a good physician, a good governor, a good grammarian, without being a good man; so that all things from without are only accessories, for the seat of it is a pure and holy mind. It consists in a congruity of actions, which we can never expect so long as we are distracted by our passions. Not but that a man may be allowed to change colour and countenance, and suffer such impressions as are properly a kind of natural force upon the body, and not under the dominion of the mind. But all this while I will have his judgement firm, and he shall act steadily and boldly, without wavering betwixt the motions of his body and those of his mind. It is not a thing indifferent, I know, whether a man lies at ease upon a bed, or in torment upon a wheel, and yet the former may be the worse of the two, if we suffer the latter with honour, and enjoy the other with infamy. It is not the *matter*, but the *virtue* that makes the action *good* or *ill*: and he that is led in triumph may be yet greater than his conqueror. When we come once to value our flesh above our honesty, we are lost. And yet I would not press upon dangers, no not so much as upon inconveniences, unless where the man and the brute come in competition. And in such a case, rather than make a forfeiture of my credit, my reason, or my faith, I would run all extremities. They are great blessings to have tender parents, dutiful children, and to live under a just and well-ordered government. Now, would it not trouble even a virtuous man, to see his children butchered before his eyes, his father made a slave, and his country over-run by a barbarous enemy? There is a great difference betwixt the simple loss of a blessing and the succeeding of a great mischief into the place of it over and above. The loss of health is followed with sickness, and the loss of sight with blindness, but this does not hold in the loss of friends and children, where there is rather something to the contrary to supply that loss; that is to say, *virtue*, which fills the mind, and takes away the desire of what we have not. What matters it whether the water be stopped or no, so long as the fountain is safe? Is a man ever the wiser for a multitude of friends, or the more foolish for the loss of them? So neither is he the happier, nor the more miserable. Short life, grief, and pain, are accessions that have no effect at all upon virtue. It consists in the action, and not in the things we do, in the choice itself, and not in the subject matter of it. It is not a despicable body, or condition, not poverty, infamy, or scandal, that can obscure the glories of virtue, but a man may see her through all oppositions, and he that looks diligently into the state of a wicked man will see the canker at his heart, through all the false and dazzling splendours of greatness and fortune. We shall then discover our *childishness* in setting our hearts upon things trivial and contemptible, and in the selling of our very country and parents for a *rattle*. And what is the difference (in effect) betwixt *old men* and *children*, but that the *one* deals in *paintings* and *statues*, and the *other* in *babies*? So that we ourselves are only the more expensive fools.

IF one could but see the mind of a good man, as it is illustrated with virtue, the beauty and the majesty of it, which is a dignity not so much as to be thought of without love and veneration, would not a man bless himself at the sight of such an object, as at the encounter of some supernatural power? A power so miraculous that it is a kind of charm upon the souls of those that are truly affected with it. There is so wonderful a grace and authority in it that even the worst of men approve it, and set up for the reputation of being accounted virtuous themselves. They covet the fruit indeed, and the profit of wickedness, but they hate, and are ashamed of the imputation of it. It is by an impression of Nature that all men have a reverence for virtue. They know it, and they have a respect for it, though they do not practise it: nay, for the countenance of their very *wickedness*, they miscall it *virtue*. Their injuries they call benefits, and expect a man should thank them for doing him a mischief; they cover their most notorious iniquities with a pretext of justice. He that robs upon

The dignity of virtue

the highway had rather find his booty than force it. Ask any of them that live upon rapine, fraud, oppression, if they had not rather enjoy a fortune honestly gotten, and their consciences will not suffer them to deny it. Men are vicious only for the profit of villainy, for at the same time that they commit it, they condemn it. Nay, so powerful is virtue, and so gracious is Providence, that every man has a light set up within him for a guide, which we do all of us both see and acknowledge, though we do not pursue it. This is it that makes the prisoner upon the torture happier than the executioner, and sickness better than health, if we bear it without yielding or repining. This is that overcomes ill fortune and moderates good; for it marches betwixt the one and the other with an equal contempt of both. It turns (like fire) all things into itself; our actions and our friendships are tinctured with it, and whatever it touches becomes amiable. That which is frail and mortal rises and falls, grows, wastes, and varies from itself, but the state of things divine is always the same. And so is virtue, let the matter be what it will. It is never the worse for the difficulty of the action, nor the better for the easiness of it. It is the same in a rich man as in a poor, in a sickly man as in a sound, in a strong as in a weak: the virtue of the besieged is as great as that of the besiegers. There are some virtues, I confess, which a good man cannot be without, and yet he had rather have no occasion to employ them. If there were any difference, I should prefer the virtues of patience before those of pleasure: for it is braver to break through difficulties than to

NO HAPPINESS WITHOUT VIRTUE

temper our delights. But, though the subject of virtue may possibly be against Nature, as to be burnt or wounded, yet the virtue itself of *an invincible patience* is according to Nature. We may seem perhaps to promise more than human nature is able to perform, but we speak with a respect to the mind, and not to the body.

IF a man does not live up to his own rules, it is something yet to have virtuous meditations and good purposes, even without acting. *The good will is accepted for the deed* It is generous, the very adventure of being good, and the bare proposal of an eminent course of life, though beyond the force of human frailty to accomplish. There is something of honour yet in the miscarriage, nay, in the naked contemplation of it. I would receive my own death with as little trouble as I would hear of another man's; I would bear the same mind, whether I be rich or poor, whether I get or lose in the world; what I have, I will not either sordidly spare, or prodigally squander away, and I will reckon upon benefits well placed as the fairest part of my possessions, not valuing them by number or weight, but by the profit and esteem of the receiver; accounting myself never the poorer for that which I give to a worthy person. What I do shall be done for conscience, not ostentation. I will eat and drink, not to gratify my palate, or only to fill and empty, but to satisfy Nature. I will be cheerful to my friends, mild, and placable to my enemies. I will prevent an honest request if I can foresee it, and I will grant it without asking. I will look upon the whole world as my country, and upon the gods, both as the witnesses and the judges of my words and deeds. I will live and die with this testimony, that I loved good studies and a good conscience; that I never invaded another man's liberty, and that I preserved my own. I will govern my life and my thoughts as if the whole world were to see the one and to read the other; for, *What does it signify to make anything a secret to my neighbour, when to God (who is the searcher of our hearts) all our privacies are open?*

VIRTUE is divided into two parts, *contemplation* and *action*. The one is delivered by institution, the other by admonition. One part of virtue consists in discipline, the other in exercise; for we must first learn, and then practise. The sooner we begin to apply ourselves to it, and the more haste we make, the longer shall we enjoy the comforts of a rectified mind; nay, we have the fruition of it in the very act of forming it; but, it is another sort of delight, I must confess, that arises from the contemplation of a soul which is advanced into the possession of wisdom and virtue. If it was so great a comfort to us to pass from the subjection of our childhood into a state of liberty and business, how much greater will it be when we come to cast off the boyish levity of our minds, and range ourselves among the philosophers? We are past our minority, it is true, but not our indiscretions; and, which is yet worse, we have the authority of seniors and the weaknesses of children (I might have said of infants, for every little thing frights the one, and every trivial fancy the other). Whoever studies this point well, will find that many things are the less to be feared, the more terrible

Virtue is divided into contemplation and action

they appear. To think anything good that is not honest, were to reproach Providence, for good men suffer inconveniences, but virtue, like the sun, goes on still with her work, let the air be never so cloudy, and finishes her course, extinguishing likewise all other splendours and oppositions, insomuch that calamity is no more to a virtuous mind than a shower into the sea. That which is right is not to be valued by *quantity*, *number*, or *time*: a life of a day may be as honest as a life of a hundred years; but yet virtue in one man may have a larger field to show itself in than in another. One man perhaps may be in a station to administer unto cities and kingdoms, to contrive good laws, create friendships, and do beneficial offices to mankind. It is another man's fortune to be straitened by poverty, or put out of the way by banishment; and yet the latter may be as virtuous as the former, and may have as great a mind, as exact a prudence, as inviolable a justice, and as large a knowledge of things both divine and human, without which a man cannot be happy. For virtue is open to all, as well to servants and exiles as to princes. It is profitable to the world and to itself, at all distances and in all conditions, and there is no difficulty can excuse a man from the exercise of it; and it is only to be found in a wise man, though there may be some faint resemblances of it in the common people. The *Stoics* hold all virtues to be equal, but yet there is a great variety in the matter they have to work upon, according as it is larger or narrower, illustrious or less noble, of more or less extent; as all good men are equal; that is to say, as they are good; but yet one may be young, another old, one may be rich, another poor, one eminent and powerful, another unknown and obscure. There are many things which have little or no grace in themselves, and are yet made glorious and remarkable by virtue. Nothing can be good which gives neither greatness nor security to the mind, but on the contrary, infects it with insolence, arrogance, and tumour. Nor does virtue dwell upon the tip of the tongue, but in the temple of a purified heart. He that depends upon any other good becomes covetous of life and what belongs to it, which exposes a man to appetites that are vast, unlimited and intolerable. Virtue is free and indefatigable, and accompanied with concord and gracefulness, whereas pleasure is mean, servile, transitory, tiresome, and sickly, and scarce outlives the tasting of it: it is the good of the belly, and not of the man, and only the felicity of brutes. Who does not know that fools enjoy their pleasures, and that there is great variety in the entertainments of wickedness? Nay, the mind itself has its variety of perverse pleasures as well as the body: as insolence, self-conceit, pride, garrulity, laziness, and the abusive wit of turning everything into *ridicule*; whereas virtue weighs all this, and corrects it. It is the knowledge both of others and of itself; it is to be learned from itself, and the very will itself may be taught; which will cannot be right unless the whole habit of the mind be right, from whence the will comes. It is by the impulse of virtue that we love virtue, so that the very way to virtue lies by virtue, which takes in also, at a view, the laws of human life.

NO HAPPINESS WITHOUT VIRTUE

NEITHER are we to value ourselves upon a day or an hour, or any one action, but upon the whole habit of the mind. Some men do one thing bravely, but not another; they will shrink at infamy, and bear up against poverty: in this case, we commend the fact and despise the man. The soul is never in the right place until it be delivered from the cares of human affairs: we must labour and climb the hill if we will arrive at virtue, whose seat is upon the top of it. He that masters avarice, and is truly good, stands firm against ambition; he looks upon his last hour, not as a punishment, but as the equity of a common fate; he that subdues his carnal lusts shall easily keep himself untainted with any other: so that reason does not encounter this or that vice by itself, but beats down all at a blow. What does he care for ignominy that only values himself upon conscience, and not opinion? *Socrates* looked a scandalous death in the face with the same constancy that he had before practised towards the Thirty Tyrants: his virtue consecrated the very dungeon; as *Cato's* repulse was *Cato's* honour, and the reproach of the government. He that is wise will take delight even in an ill opinion that is well gotten; it is ostentation, not virtue, when a man will have his good deeds published; and it is not enough to be just where there is honour to be gotten, but to continue so, in defiance of infamy and danger.

A virtuous life must be all of a piece

BUT virtue cannot lie hid, for the time will come that shall raise it again (even after it is buried) and deliver it from the malignity of the age that oppressed it. Immortal glory is the shadow of it, and keeps it company whether we will or no; but sometimes the shadow goes before the substance, and other-whiles it follows it: and the later it comes, the larger it is, when envy itself shall have given way to it. It was a long time that *Democritus* was taken for a madman, and before *Socrates* had any esteem in the world. How long was it before *Cato* could be understood? Nay, he was affronted, condemned and rejected; and people never knew the value of him until they had lost him. The integrity and courage of mad *Rutilius* had been forgotten, but for his sufferings. I speak of those that fortune has made famous for their persecutions. And there are others also that the world never took notice of until they were dead; as *Epicurus* and *Metrodorus*, that were almost wholly unknown, even in the place where they lived. Now, as the body is to be kept in upon the downhill, and forced upwards, so there are some virtues that require the rein, and others the spur. In *liberality*, *temperance*, *gentleness of nature*, we are to check ourselves, for fear of falling; but in *patience*, *resolution*, and *perseverance*, where we are to mount the hill, we stand in need of encouragement. Upon this division of the matter I had rather steer the smoother course than pass through the experiments of sweat and blood: I know it is my duty to be content in all conditions, but yet, if it were at my election, I would choose the fairest. When a

Virtue can never be suppressed

man comes once to stand in need of fortune, his life is anxious, suspicious, timorous, dependent upon every moment, and in fear of all accidents. How can that man resign himself to God, or bear his lot, whatever it be, without murmuring, and cheerfully submit to Providence, that shrinks at every motion of pleasure or pain? It is virtue alone that raises us above griefs, hopes, fears and chances, and makes us not only patient, but willing, as knowing that whatever we suffer is according to the decree of heaven. He that is overcome with pleasure (so contemptible and weak an enemy) – what will become of him when he comes to grapple with dangers, necessities, torments, death, and the dissolution of Nature itself? Wealth, honour, and favour may come upon a man by chance; nay, they may be cast upon him without so much as looking after them: but virtue is the work of industry and labour; and certainly it is worth the while to purchase that good which brings all others along with it. A good man is happy within himself, and independent upon fortune, kind to his friend, temperate to his enemy, religiously just, indefatigably laborious; and he discharges all duties with a constancy and congruity of actions.

CHAPTER 4

PHILOSOPHY IS THE GUIDE OF LIFE

IF it be true that the *understanding* and the *will* are the *two eminent faculties of the reasonable soul*, it follows necessarily that wisdom and virtue (which are the best improvements of these two faculties) must be the perfection also of our *reasonable being*, and consequently *the undeniable foundation of a happy life*. There is not any duty to which Providence has not annexed a blessing, nor any institution of heaven which, even in this life, we may not be the better for; nor any temptation, either of fortune or of appetite, that is not subject to our reason; nor any passion or affliction for which virtue has not provided a remedy. So that it is our own fault if we either fear or hope for anything – which two affections are the root of all our miseries. From this general prospect of the *foundation* of our *tranquillity*, we shall pass by degrees to a particular consideration of the *means* by which it may be *procured*, and of the *impediments* that *obstruct* it, beginning with that *philosophy* which principally regards our *manners*, and instructs us in the measures of a virtuous and quiet life.

PHILOSOPHY is divided into *moral, natural,* and rational. The *first* concerns our *manners,* the *second* searches the works of *Nature*, and the *third* furnishes us with propriety of *words* and *arguments*, and the faculty of *distinguishing*,

<small>Philosophy is moral, natural, and rational</small>

that we may not be imposed upon with tricks and fallacies. The *causes* of things fall under *natural philosophy*, *arguments* under *rational*, and *actions* under *moral*. *Moral philosophy* is again divided into matter of *justice*, which arises from the estimation of things and of men; and into *affections* and *actions*; and a failing in any one of these disorders all the rest. For what does it profit us to know the true value of things if we be transported by our passions? Or to master our appetites without understanding the *when*, the *what*, the *how*, and other circumstances of our proceedings? For it is one thing to know the rate and dignity of things, and another to know the little nicks and springs of acting. *Natural philosophy* is conversant about things *corporeal* and *incorporeal*, the disquisition of *causes* and *effects*, and the contemplation of the *cause of causes*. *Rational philosophy* is divided into *logic* and *rhetoric*; the one looks after *words*, *sense*, and *order*; the other treats barely of *words*, and the *significations* of them. *Socrates* places all *philosophy in morals*, and *wisdom* in the distinguishing of *good* and *evil*. It is the art and law of life, and it teaches us what to do in all cases, and, like good marksmen, to hit the white at any distance. The force of it is incredible, for it gives us in the weakness of a man the security of a *spirit*: in sickness, it is as good as a remedy to us; for whatsoever eases the mind is profitable also to the body. The *physician* may prescribe diet and exercise, and accommodate his rule and medicine to the disease, but it is *philosophy* that must bring us to a contempt of death, which is the remedy of all diseases. In poverty it gives us riches, or such a state of mind as makes them superfluous to us. It arms us against all difficulties: one man is pressed with death, another with poverty, some with envy; others are offended at Providence, and unsatisfied with the condition of mankind. But *philosophy* prompts us to relieve the prisoner, the infirm, the necessitous, the condemned, to show the ignorant their errors, and rectify their affections. It makes us inspect and govern our manners; it rouses us where we are faint and drowsy; it binds up what is loose, and humbles in us that which is contumacious. It delivers the mind from the bondage of the body, and raises it up to the contemplation of its divine original. Honours, monuments, and all the works of vanity and ambition are demolished and destroyed by time, but the reputation of wisdom is venerable to posterity; and those that were envied or neglected in their lives are adored in their memories, and exempted from the very laws of created Nature, which has set bounds to all other things. The very shadow of *glory* carries a man of *honour* upon all dangers, to the contempt of fire and sword; and it were a shame if *right reason* should not inspire as generous resolutions into a man of *virtue*.

NEITHER is *philosophy* only profitable to the public, but one wise man helps another, even in the exercise of their virtues; and the one has need of the other, both for conversation and counsel; for they kindle a mutual emulation in good offices. We are not so perfect yet, but that many new things remain still to be found out, which will give us the reciprocal advantages of

One wise man teaches another

instructing one another. For, as one wicked man is contagious to another, and the more vices are mingled, the worse it is, so is it on the contrary with good men and their virtues. As men of letters are the most useful and excellent of friends, so are they the best of subjects – as being better judges of the blessings they enjoy under a well ordered government, and of what they owe to the magistrate for their freedom and protection. They are men of sobriety and learning, and free from boasting and insolence. They reprove the vice without reproaching the person, for they have learned to be wise without either pomp or envy. That which we see in high mountains we find in *philosophers*; they seem taller near hand than at a distance. They are raised above other men, but their greatness is substantial. Nor do they stand upon the tiptoe that they may seem higher than they are, but content with their own stature, they reckon themselves tall enough when fortune cannot reach them. Their laws are short, and yet comprehensive too, for they bind all.

IT is the bounty of *Nature* that we *live*, but of *philosophy* that we *live well,* which is in truth a greater benefit than life itself. Not but that *philosophy* is also the gift of heaven, so far as to the faculty, but not to the science; for that must be the business of industry. No man is born wise. But wisdom and virtue require a tutor, though we can easily learn to be vicious without a master. It is *philosophy* that gives us a veneration for God, a charity for our neighbour, that teaches us our duty to heaven, and exhorts us to an agreement one with another. It unmasks

Philosophy teaches us to live well

things that are terrible to us, assuages our lusts, refutes our errors, restrains our luxury, reproves our avarice, and works strangely upon tender natures. I could never hear *Attalus* (says *Seneca*) upon the vices of the age and the errors of life, without a compassion for mankind; and in his discourses upon poverty there was something, methought, that was more than human. *More than we use*, says he, *is more than we need, and only a burden to the bearer.* That saying of his put me out of countenance at the superfluities of my own fortune. And so in his invectives against vain pleasures, he did at such a rate advance the felicities of a sober table, a pure mind and a chaste body, that a man could not hear him without a love for continence and moderation. Upon these lectures of his, I denied myself, for a while after, certain delicacies that I had formerly used: but, in a short time, I fell to them again, though so sparingly that the proportion came little short of a total abstinence.

NOW, to show you (says our Author) how much more earnest my entrance upon philosophy was than my progress, my tutor *Sotion* gave me a wonderful kindness for *Pythagoras*, and after him for *Sextius*. The former forbore shedding of blood, upon his *metempsychosis*; and put men in fear of it, lest they should offer violence to the souls of some of their departed friends or relations. *Whether*, says he, *there be a transmigration or not, if it be true, there is no hurt in it; if false, there is frugality. And nothing is gotten by cruelty neither, but the cozening a wolf, perhaps, or a vulture of a supper.* Now, *Sextius* abstained

Youth is apt to take good impressions

upon another account, which was that *he would not have men inured to hardness of heart by the laceration and tormenting of living creatures; beside, that Nature had sufficiently provided for the sustenance of mankind, without blood.* This wrought so far upon me that I gave over eating of flesh, and in one year made it not only easy to me, but pleasant; my mind, methought, was more at liberty (and I am still of the same opinion), but I gave it over nevertheless, and the reason was this – it was imputed as a superstition to the *Jews*, the forbearance of some sorts of flesh, and my father brought me back again to my old custom, that I might not be thought tainted with their superstition. Nay, and I had much ado to prevail upon myself to suffer it too. I make use of this instance to show the aptness of youth to take good impressions, if there be a friend at hand to press them. Philosophers are the tutors of mankind; if they have found out remedies for the mind, it must be our part to apply them. I cannot think of *Cato*, *Lelius*, *Socrates*, *Plato*, without veneration; their very names are sacred to me. Philosophy is the health of the mind; let us look to that health first, and in the second place to that of the body, which may be had upon easier terms, for a strong arm, a robust constitution, or the skill of procuring this, is not a philosopher's business. He does some things as *a wise man*, and other things as he is a *man*; and he may have strength of body as well as of mind; but if he runs or casts the sledge, it were injurious to ascribe that to his wisdom which is common to the greatest of fools. He studies rather to fill his mind than his coffers, and he knows that gold and silver were mingled with dirt, until avarice or ambition parted them. His life is ordinate, fearless, equal, secure; he stands firm in all extremities, and bears the lot of his humanity with a divine temper. There is a great difference betwixt the splendour of philosophy and of fortune; the one shines with an original light, the other with a borrowed one; beside that it makes us happy and immortal, for learning shall outlive palaces and monuments. The house of a wise man is safe, though narrow; there is neither noise nor furniture in it, no porter at the door, nor anything that is either vendible or mercenary, nor any business of fortune; for she has nothing to do where she has nothing to look after. This is the way to heaven, which Nature has chalked out, and it is both secure and pleasant; there needs no train of servants, no pomp or equipage, to make good our passage; no money or letters of credit for expenses upon the voyage, but the graces of an honest mind will serve us upon the way, and make us happy at our journey's end.

TO tell you my opinion now of the *liberal sciences*; I have no great esteem for anything that terminates in profit or money, and yet I shall allow them to be so far beneficial as they only *prepare* the understanding without *detaining* it. They are but the rudiments of wisdom, and only then to be learned when the mind is capable of nothing better, and the knowledge of them is better worth the keeping than the acquiring. They do not so much as pretend to the making of us virtuous, but only to give us an aptitude of

The liberal sciences are matters rather of curiosity than virtue

disposition to be so. The *grammarian's* business lies in a *syntax* of speech, or if he proceed to *history*, or the measuring of a *verse*, he is at the end of his line. But what signifies a congruity of periods, the computing of syllables or the modifying of numbers, to the taming of our passions or the repressing of our lusts? The *philosopher* proves the body of the sun to be large, but for the true dimensions of it we must ask the *mathematician*. *Geometry* and *music*, if they do not teach us to master our hopes and fears, all the rest is to little purpose. What does it concern us which was the elder of the two, *Homer* or *Hesiod*? Or which was the taller, *Helen* or *Hecuba*? We take a great deal of pains to trace *Ulysses* in his wanderings. But were it not time as well spent to look to ourselves, that we may not wander at all? Are not we ourselves tossed with tempestuous passions? And both *assaulted* by terrible *monsters* on the one hand, and *tempted* by *sirens* on the other? Teach me my duty to my country, to my father, to my wife, to mankind. What is it to me whether *Penelope* was *honest* or no? Teach me to know how to be so myself, and to live according to that knowledge. What am I the better for putting so many parts together in *music*, and raising a harmony out of so many different tones? Teach me to tune my affections, and to hold constant to myself. *Geometry* teaches me the art of *measuring acres*; teach me to *measure my appetites*, and to know when I have enough. Teach me to divide with my brother, and to rejoice in the prosperity of my neighbour. You teach me how I may hold my own and keep my estate, but I would rather learn how I may lose it all, and yet be contented. *It is hard*, you will say, *for a man to be forced from the fortune of his family*. This estate, it is true, was my *father's*, but whose was it in the time of my *great grandfather*? I do not only say, What *man's* was it? but What *nation's*? The *astrologer* tells me of *Saturn* and *Mars* in *opposition*, but I say, let them be as they will, their courses and their positions are ordered them by an unchangeable decree of Fate. Either they produce and point out the effects of all things, or else they signify them. If the former, what are we the better for the knowledge of that which must of necessity come to pass? If the latter, what does it avail us to foresee what we cannot avoid? So that whether we know or not know, the event will still be the same.

HE that designs the institution of human life should not be over-curious of his words; it does not stand with his dignity to be solicitous about sounds and syllables, and to debase the mind of man with small and trivial things, placing wisdom in matters that are rather difficult than great. If it be *eloquent*, it is his *good fortune*, not his *business*. Subtle disputations are only the sport of wits that play upon the catch, and are fitter to be condemned than resolved. Were not I a madman to sit wrangling about words and putting of nice and impertinent questions, when the enemy has already made the breach, the town fired over my head, and the mine ready to play, that shall blow me up into the air? Were this a time for fooleries? Let me rather fortify myself against death and in-

It is not for the dignity of a philosopher to be curious about words

evitable necessities, let me understand that the good of life does not consist in the length or space, but in the use of it. When I go to *sleep*, who knows whether ever I shall *wake* again? And when I *wake*, whether ever I shall *sleep* again? When I go *abroad*, whether ever I shall come *home* again? And when I *return*, whether ever I shall go *abroad* again? It is not at sea only that life and death are within a few inches of one another, but they are as near everywhere else too, only we do not take so much notice of it. What have we to do with frivolous and captious questions and impertinent niceties? Let us rather study how to deliver ourselves from sadness, fear, and the burden of all our secret lusts. Let us pass over all our most solemn levities and make haste to a good life, which is a thing that presses us. Shall a man that goes for a midwife stand gaping upon a post to see *what play today*? Or, when his house is on fire, stay the curling of a periwig before he calls for help? Our houses are on fire, our country invaded, our goods taken away, our children in danger, and, I might add to these, the calamities of earthquakes, shipwrecks, and whatever else is most terrible. Is this a time for us now to be playing fast and loose with idle questions which are, in effect, but so many unprofitable riddles? Our duty is the cure of the mind rather than the delight of it; but we have only the words of wisdom without the works, and turn philosophy into a pleasure, that was given for a remedy. What can be more ridiculous than for a man to *neglect* his *manners* and *compose* his *style*? We are sick and ulcerous, and must be lanced and scarified, and every man has as much business within himself as a physician in a common pestilence. *Misfortunes, in fine, cannot be avoided; but they may be sweetened, if not overcome, and our lives may be made happy by philosophy.*

CHAPTER 5

THE FORCE OF PRECEPTS

THERE seems to be so near an affinity betwixt *wisdom, philosophy,* and *good counsels,* that it is rather a matter of curiosity than of profit to divide them; *philosophy* being only a *limited wisdom,* and *good counsels a communication of that wisdom* for the good of *others,* as well as of *ourselves;* and to *posterity,* as well as to the *present.* The *wisdom* of the *ancients,* as to the government of life, was no more than certain precepts what to do, and what not; and men were much better in that simplicity, for as they came to be more *learned,* they grew less careful of being *good.* That *plain* and *open virtue* is now turned into a *dark* and *intricate science,* and we are taught to *dispute* rather than to *live.* So long as wickedness was simple, simple remedies also were sufficient against it; but now it has taken root and spread, we must make use of stronger.

THERE are some dispositions that embrace good things as soon as they hear them, but they will still need quickening by admonition and precept. We are rash and forward in some cases, and dull in others. And there is no repressing of the one humour, or raising of the other, but by removing the causes of them, which are (in one word) *false admiration* and *false fear.* Every man knows his duty to his country, to his friends, to his guests; and yet when he is called upon to draw his sword for the one, or to labour for the

The best of us are yet the better for admonition and precept

other, he finds himself distracted betwixt his apprehensions and his delights. He knows well enough the injury he does his wife in the keeping of a wench, and yet his lust overrules him: so that it is not enough to give good advice, unless we can take away that which hinders the benefit of it. If a man does what he ought to do, he will never do it constantly, or equally, without knowing why he does it. And if it be only chance or custom, he that does well by chance may do ill so too. And farther, a precept may direct us what we *ought* to do, and yet fall short in the manner of doing it. An expensive entertainment may, in one case, be extravagance or gluttony, and yet a point of honour and discretion in another. *Tiberius Caesar* had a huge *mullet* presented him, which he sent to the market to be sold: *And now*, says he, *my masters* (to some company with him), *you shall see that either* Apricius *or* Octavius *will be the chapman for this fish.* Octavius beat the price, and gave about thirty pounds *sterling* for it. Now, there was a great difference between *Octavius*, that bought it for his luxury, and the *other* that purchased it for a *compliment* to *Tiberius*. Precepts are idle if we be not first taught what opinion we are to have of the matter in question; whether it be *poverty, riches, disgrace, sickness, banishment, &c.* Let us therefore examine them one by one, not what they are *called*, but what in truth they *are*. And so for the *virtues*: it is to no purpose to set a high esteem upon *prudence, fortitude, temperance* and *justice*, if we do not first know *what virtue is*, whether *one* or *more*, or if he that has *one* has *all*, or *how they differ*.

THE FORCE OF PRECEPTS

PRECEPTS are of great weight, and a few useful ones at hand do more toward a happy life than whole volumes of cautions that we know not where to find. These solitary precepts should be our daily meditation, for they are the rules by which we ought to square our lives. When they are contracted into *sentences*, they strike the *affections*, whereas *admonition* is only *blowing of the coal*; it moves the vigour of the mind and excites virtue: we have the thing already, but we know not where it lies. It is by precepts that the understanding is nourished and augmented; the offices of prudence and justice are guided by them, and they lead us to the execution of our duties. A *precept* delivered in *verse* has a much greater effect than in *prose*; and those very people that never think they have enough, let them but hear a sharp sentence against *avarice*, how will they clap and admire it, and bid open defiance to money? So soon as we find the affections struck, we must follow the blow, not with *syllogisms* or quirks of *wit*, but with *plain* and *weighty reason*: and we must do it with *kindness* too, and *respect*, for *there goes a blessing along with counsels and discourses that are bent wholly upon the good of the hearer*. And those are still the most efficacious that take reason along with them, and tell us as well *why* we are to do this or that, as *what* we are to do. For some understandings are weak and need an instructor to expound to them what is good and what is evil. It is a great virtue to *love*, to *give*, and to *follow good counsel*; if it does not lead us to honesty, it does at least *prompt* us to it. As several parts make up but one harmony,

The power of precepts and sentences

and the most agreeable music arises from discords, so should a wise man gather many acts, many precepts, and the examples of many arts, to inform his own life. Our forefathers have left us in charge to avoid three things: *hatred, envy,* and *contempt*. Now, it is hard to avoid *envy* and not incur *contempt*; for in taking too much care not to usurp upon others, we become many times liable to be trampled upon ourselves. Some people are afraid of others because it is possible that others may be afraid of them: but let us secure ourselves on all hands; for *flattery* is as dangerous as *contempt*. It is not to say, in case of *admonition, I knew this before*: for we know many things, but we do not think of them; so that it is the part of a *monitor* not so much to *teach* as to *mind* us of our duties. Sometimes a man oversees that which lies just under his nose; otherwhile he is careless, or *pretends* not to see it. We do all know that friendship is sacred, and yet we violate it; and the greatest libertine expects that his own wife should be honest.

GOOD counsel is the most needful service that we can do to mankind, and if we give it to many, it will be sure to profit *some*. For, of many trials, some or other will undoubtedly succeed. He that places a man in the possession of himself does a great thing, for wisdom does not show itself so much in precept as in life, in a firmness of mind and a mastery of appetite. It teaches us to *do* as well as to *talk*, and to make our words and actions all of a colour. If that fruit be most pleasant which we gather from a tree of our own planting, how

Good counsel is the best service we can do to mankind

THE FORCE OF PRECEPTS

much greater delight shall we take in the growth and increase of good manners of our own forming? It is an eminent mark of wisdom for a man to be always like himself. You shall have some that keep a thrifty table, and lash out upon building; profuse upon themselves, and forbid to others; niggardly at home, and lavish abroad. This diversity is vicious, and the effect of a dissatisfied and uneasy mind; whereas every wise man lives by rule. This disagreement of purposes arises from hence, either that we do not propound to ourselves what we would be at, or if we do, that we do not pursue it, but pass from one thing to another: and we do not only *change* neither, but return to the very thing which we had both quitted and condemned.

IN all our undertakings, let us first examine our own strength, the enterprise next, and thirdly, the persons with whom we have to do. The first point is most important, for we are apt to over-value ourselves *Three points to be examined in all our undertakings* and reckon that we can do more than indeed we can. One man sets up for a speaker, and is out as soon as he opens his mouth; another overcharges his estate perhaps, or his body. A bashful man is not fit for public business. Some again are too stiff and peremptory for the court. Many people are apt to fly out in their anger, nay, and in a frolic too; if any sharp thing fall in their way, they will rather venture a neck than lose a jest. These people had better be quiet in the world than busy. Let him that is naturally choleric and impatient avoid all provocations and those affairs also that multiply and draw on more, and those also from which there is no retreat. When we may come off at pleasure, and fairly hope to bring our matters to a period, it is well enough. If it so happen that a man be tied up to business which he can neither loosen nor break off, let him imagine those shackles upon his mind to be irons upon his legs: they are troublesome at first, but when there is no remedy but patience, custom makes them easy to us, and necessity gives us courage. We are all slaves to fortune; some only in loose and golden chains, others in strait ones and coarser. Nay, and *they that bind us are slaves too themselves*, some to honour, others to wealth, some to offices, others to contempt; some to their superiors, others to themselves. Nay, life itself is a servitude. Let us make the best of it then, and with our philosophy mend our fortune. Difficulties may be softened, and heavy burdens disposed of to our ease. Let us covet nothing out of our reach, but content ourselves with things hopeful and at hand, and without envying the advantages of others. For greatness stands upon a craggy precipice, and it is much safer and quieter living upon a level. How many great men are forced to keep their station upon mere necessity, because they find there is no coming down from it but headlong? These men would do well to fortify themselves against ill consequences by such virtues and meditations as may make them less solicitous for the future. The surest expedient in this case is to bound our desires, and to leave nothing to fortune which we may keep in our own power. Neither will this course wholly

THE FORCE OF PRECEPTS

compose us, but it shows us, at worst, the end of our troubles.

IT is a main point to take care that we propose nothing but what is hopeful and honest. For it will be equally troublesome to us, either not to succeed, or to be ashamed of the success. Wherefore, let us be sure not to admit any ill designs into our heart, that we may lift up pure hands to heaven, and ask nothing which another shall be a loser by. Let us pray for a good mind, which is a wish to no man's injury. I will remember always that I am a man, and then consider, that if I am *happy*, it will not last *always*; if *unhappy*, I may be *other* if I please. I will carry my life in my hand, and deliver it up readily when it shall be called for. I will have a care of being a slave to myself, for it is a perpetual, a shameful, and the heaviest of all servitudes; and this may be done by moderate desires. I will say to myself, *What is it that I labour, sweat, and solicit for, when it is but very little that I want, and it will not be long that I shall need anything?* He that would make a trial of the firmness of his mind, let him set certain days apart for the practice of his virtues. Let him mortify himself with fasting, coarse clothes and hard lodging, and then say to himself, *Is this the thing now that I was afraid of?* In a state of security a man may thus prepare himself against hazards, and in plenty fortify himself against want. If you will have a man resolute when he comes to the push, train him up to it beforehand. The soldier does duty in peace that he may be in breath when he comes to battle. How many great and wise men have made

Propose nothing but what is hopeful and honest

experiment of their moderation by a practice of abstinence, to the highest degree of hunger and thirst, and convinced themselves that a man may fill his belly without being beholden to fortune, which never denies any of us wherewith to satisfy our necessities, though she be never so angry? It is as easy to *suffer* it *always* as to *try* it *once*; and it is no more than thousands of servants and poor people do every day of their lives. He that would live happily must neither trust to good fortune nor submit to bad. He must stand upon his guard against all assaults. He must stick to himself, without any dependence upon other people. Where the mind is tinctured with philosophy there is no place for grief, anxiety, or superfluous vexations. It is prepossessed with virtue, to the neglect of fortune, which brings us to a degree of security not to be disturbed. It is easier to give counsel than to take it, and a common thing for one choleric man to condemn another. We may be sometimes earnest in advising, but not violent or tedious. Few words with gentleness and efficacy are best. The misery is, that the wise do not need counsel, and fools will not take it. A good man, it is true, delights in it: and it is a mark of folly and ill nature to hate reproof. To a friend I would be always frank and plain, and rather fail in the success than be wanting in the matter of faith and trust. There are some precepts that serve in common, both to the rich and poor, but they are too general; as *Cure your avarice, and the work is done*. It is one thing not to desire money, and another thing not to understand how to use it. In the choice of the persons we have to do withal, we should see that

THE FORCE OF PRECEPTS

they be worth our while; in the choice of our business we are to consult Nature, and follow our inclinations. He that gives sober advice to a witty droll must look to have everything turned into ridicule. *As if you philosophers*, says Marcellinus, *did not love your whores and your guts as well as other people*; and then he tells you of such and such that were taken in the manner. We are all sick, I must confess, and it is not for sick men to play the physicians, but it is yet lawful for a man in a hospital to discourse of the common condition and distempers of the place. He that should pretend to teach a madman how to speak, walk, and behave himself, were he not the madder man of the two? He that directs the pilot, makes him move the helm, order the sails so or so, and make the best of a scant wind, after this or that manner. And so should we do in our counsels. Do not tell me what a man should do in health or poverty, but show me the way to be either sound or rich. Teach me to master my vices. For it is to no purpose, so long as I am under their government, to tell me what I must do when I am clear of it. In case of an avarice a little eased, a luxury moderated, a temerity restrained, a sluggish humour quickened, precepts will then help us forward, and tutor us how to behave ourselves. It is the first and the main tie of a soldier, his military oath, which is an engagement upon him both of religion and honour. In like manner, he that pretends to a happy life must first lay a foundation of virtue as a bond upon him, to live and die true to that cause. We do not find felicity in the veins of the earth where we dig for gold, nor in the bottom of the sea where we fish for pearl, but in a pure and untainted mind, which, if it were not holy, were not fit to entertain the deity. *He that would be truly happy must think his own lot best, and so live with men, as considering that God sees him, and so speak to God as if men heard him.*

CHAPTER 6

NO FELICITY LIKE PEACE OF CONSCIENCE

A GOOD *conscience is the testimony of a good life, and the reward of it.* This is it that fortifies the mind against fortune, when a man has gotten the mastery of his passions, placed his treasure and his security within himself, learned to be content with his condition and that death is no evil in itself, but only the end of man. He that has dedicated his mind to virtue and to the good of human society, whereof he is a member, has consummated all that is either profitable or necessary for him to know, or do, toward the establishment of his peace. Every man has a judge and a witness within himself, of all the good and ill that he does, which inspires us with great thoughts, and administers to us wholesome counsels. We have a veneration for all the works of Nature, the heads of rivers, and the springs of medicinal waters: the horrors of groves and of caves strike us with an impression of religion and worship. To see a man fearless in dangers, untainted with lusts, happy in adversity, composed in a tumult, and laughing at all those things which are generally either coveted or feared; all men must acknowledge that this can be nothing else but a beam of divinity that influences a mortal body. And this is it that carries us to the disquisition of things divine and human; what the state of the world was before the distribution of the first matter into parts; what power it was that drew order out of that confusion, and gave laws both to the whole and to every particle thereof; what that space is beyond the world, and whence proceed the several operations of Nature. Shall any man see the glory and order of the universe; so many scattered parts and qualities wrought into one mass; such a medley of things, which are yet distinguished; the world enlightened, and the disorders of it so wonderfully regulated; and shall he not consider the Author and Disposer of all this; and whither we ourselves shall go when our souls shall be delivered from the slavery of our flesh? The whole creation, we see, conforms to the dictates of Providence, and follows God both as a governor and as a guide. A great, a good, and a right mind, is a kind of divinity lodged in flesh, and may be the blessing of a slave as well as of a prince; it came from heaven, and to heaven it must return; and it is a kind of heavenly felicity which a pure and virtuous mind enjoys in some degree, even upon earth: whereas temples of honour are but empty names, which probably owe their beginning either to ambition or to violence. I am strangely transported with the thoughts of eternity, nay, with the belief of it; for I have a profound veneration for the opinions of great men, especially when they promise things so much to my satisfaction – for they do promise them, though they do not prove them. In the question of the immortality of the soul, it goes very far with me, a general consent to the opinion of a future reward and punishment, which meditation raises me to the contempt of this life, in hopes of a better. But still, though we know that we

PEACE OF CONSCIENCE

have a soul, yet what the soul is, how, and from whence, we are utterly ignorant. This only we understand, that all the good and ill we do is under the dominion of the mind; that a clear conscience states us in an inviolable peace: and that the greatest blessing in Nature is that which every honest man may bestow upon himself. The body is but the clog and prisoner of the mind, tossed up and down, and persecuted with punishments, violences, and diseases; but the mind itself is sacred and eternal, and exempt from the danger of all actual impressions.

PROVIDED that we look to our consciences, no matter for opinion. Let me deserve well, though I hear ill. The common people take stomach and audacity for the marks of magnanimity and honour; and, if a man be soft and modest, they look upon him as an easy fop: but when they come once to observe the dignity of his mind in the equality and firmness of his actions, and that his external quiet is founded upon an internal peace, the very same people have him in esteem and admiration. For there is no man but approves of virtue, though but few pursue it; we see where it is, but we dare not venture to come at it. And the reason is, we overvalue that which we must quit to obtain it. A good conscience fears no witnesses, but a guilty conscience is solicitous, even in solitude. If we do nothing but what is honest, let all the world know it; but if otherwise, what does it signify to have nobody else know it, so long as I know it myself? Miserable is he that slights that witness! Wickedness, it is true, may escape the

Every man's conscience is his judge

law, but not the conscience. For a private conviction is the first and the greatest punishment of offenders; so that sin plagues itself, and the fear of vengeance pursues even those that escape the stroke of it. It were ill for good men that iniquity may so easily evade the law, the judge, and the execution, if Nature had not set up torments and gibbets in the consciences of transgressors. He that is guilty lives in perpetual terror, and while he expects to be punished, he punishes himself; and, whosoever deserves it, expects it. What if he be not detected? He is still in apprehension yet that he may be so. His sleeps are painful and never secure; and he cannot speak of another man's wickedness without thinking of his own; whereas a good conscience is a continual feast. Those are the only certain and profitable delights which arise from the conscience of a well-acted life. No matter for noise abroad, so long as we are quiet within: but if our passions be seditious, that is enough to keep us waking, without any other tumult. It is not the posture of the body, or the composure of the bed, that will give rest to an uneasy mind. There is an impatient sloth that may be roused by action, and the vices of laziness must be cured by business. True happiness is not to be found in excesses of wine, or of women, nor in the largest prodigalities of fortune. What she has given me, she may take away, but she shall not tear it from me; and so long as it does not grow to me, I can part with it without pain. He that would perfectly know himself, let him set aside his money, his fortune, his dignity,

PEACE OF CONSCIENCE

and examine himself naked, without being put to learn from others the knowledge of himself.

IT is dangerous for a man too suddenly or too easily to believe himself. Wherefore let us examine, watch, observe, and inspect our own hearts, for we ourselves are our own greatest flatterers. We should every night call ourselves to an account, *What infirmity have I mastered today? What passion opposed? What temptation resisted? What virtue acquired?* Our vices will abate of themselves, if they be brought every day to the shrift. Oh the blessed sleep that follows such a diary! Oh the tranquillity, liberty, and greatness of that mind that is a spy upon itself, and a private censor of its own manners! It is my custom (says our Author) every night, so soon as the candle is out, to run over all the words and actions of the past day, and I let nothing escape me; for why should I fear the sight of my own errors, when I can admonish and forgive myself? *I was a little too hot in such a dispute: my opinion might have been as well spared, for it gave offence, and did no good at all. The thing was true, but all truths are not to be spoken at all times; I would I had held my tongue, for there is no contending either with fools, or our superiors. I have done ill, but it shall be so no more.* If every man would but thus look into himself, it would be the better for us all. What can be more reasonable than this daily review of a life that we cannot warrant for a moment? Our fate is set, and the first breath we draw is only the first motion toward our last. One cause depends upon another, and the

Let every man examine himself

course of all things, public and private, is but a long connection of Providential appointments. There is a great variety in our lives, but all tends to the same issue. *Nature* may use her own bodies as she pleases, but a good man has this consolation, that nothing perishes which he can call his own. It is a great comfort that we are only condemned to the same fate with the universe; the heavens themselves are mortal, as well as our bodies; Nature has made us passive, and to suffer is our lot. While we are in flesh, every man has his chain and his clog, and it is looser and lighter to one man than to another; only he is more at ease that takes it up and carries it, than he that drags it. We are born to lose and to perish, to hope and to fear, to vex ourselves and others; and there is no antidote against a common calamity, but virtue; for *the foundation of true joy is in the conscience.*

CHAPTER 7

A GOOD MAN CAN NEVER BE MISERABLE, NOR A WICKED MAN HAPPY

THERE is not in the scale of nature a more inseparable connection of cause and effect than in the case of happiness and virtue, nor anything that more naturally produces the one, or more necessarily presupposes the other. For what is it to be happy, but for a man to content himself with his lot in a cheerful and quiet resignation to the appointments of God? All the actions of our lives ought to be governed with a respect to good and evil: and it is only reason that distinguishes, by which reason we are in such a manner influenced, as if a ray of the divinity were dipped in a mortal body, and that is the perfection of mankind. It is true, we have not the eyes of eagles nor the sagacity of hounds, nor if we had could we pretend to value ourselves upon anything which we have in common with brutes. What are we the better for that which is foreign to us, and may be given and taken away? As the beams of the Sun irradiate the Earth, and yet remain where they were, so is it in some proportion with a holy mind that illustrates all our actions and yet adheres to its original. Why do we not as well commend a horse for his glorious trappings, as a man for his pompous additions? How much a braver creature is a lion (which by Nature ought to be fierce and terrible), how much braver (I say) in his natural horror than in his chains? So that everything in its pure nature pleases us best. It is not health, nobility or riches that can justify a wicked man, nor is it the want of all these that can discredit a good one. That is the sovereign blessing which makes the possessor of it valuable without anything else, and him that wants it contemptible, though he had all the world besides. It is not the painting, gilding or carving that makes a good ship, but if she be a nimble sailer, tight and strong, to endure the seas, that is her excellency. It is the edge and temper of the blade that makes a good sword, not the richness of the scabbard: and so it is not money, or possessions, that make a man considerable, but his virtue.

IT is every man's duty to make himself profitable to mankind. If he can, to many; if not, to fewer. If not so neither, to his neighbours; but however to himself.

A good man makes himself profitable to mankind

There are two republics, a great one, which is human nature, and a less, which is the place where we were born. Some serve both at a time, some only the greater, and some again only the less. The greater may be served in privacy, solitude, contemplation, and perchance, that way better than any other; but it was the intent of Nature, however, that we should serve both. A good man may serve the public, his friend, and himself, in any station. If he be not for the sword, let him take the gown; if the bar does not agree with him, let him try the pulpit; if he be silenced abroad, let him give counsel at home, and discharge the part of a faithful friend and a temperate companion. When he is

A GOOD MAN CAN NEVER BE MISERABLE

no longer a citizen, he is yet a man; the whole world is his country, and human nature never wants matter to work upon. But if nothing will serve a man in the *civil government* unless he be *prime minister*, or in the *field*, but to *command in chief*, it is his own fault. The common soldier, where he cannot use his hands, fights with his very looks, his example, his encouragement, his voice, and stands his ground even when he has lost his hands, and does service too with his very clamour, so that in any condition whatsoever, he still discharges the duty of a good patriot. Nay, he that spends his time well, even in a retirement, gives a great example. We may enlarge indeed, or contract, according to the circumstances of time, place, or abilities, but above all things we must be sure to keep ourselves in action, for he that is slothful is dead even while he lives. Was there ever any state so desperate as that of *Athens* under the *Thirty Tyrants*, where it was capital to be honest, and the Senate House was turned into a College of Hangmen? Never was any government so wretched and so hopeless: and yet *Socrates* at the same time preached *temperance* to the *tyrants*, and *courage* to the *rest*: and afterwards died an eminent example of faith and resolution, and a sacrifice for the common good.

IT is not for a wise man to stand shifting and fencing with fortune, but to oppose her barefaced, for he is sufficiently convinced that she can do him no hurt. She may take away his servants, possessions and dignity, assault his body, put out his eyes, cut off his hands and strip him of all the external comforts of life. But what

The injuries of Fortune do not affect the mind

does all this amount to, more than the recalling of a trust which he has received, with condition to deliver it up again upon demand? He looks upon himself as precarious, and only lent to himself, and yet he does not value himself ever the less because he is not his own, but takes such care as an honest man should do of a thing that is committed to him in trust. Whensoever he that lent me myself and what I have shall call for all back again, it is not a loss, but a restitution, and I must willingly deliver up what most undeservedly was bestowed upon me. And it will become me to return my mind better than I received it.

DEMETRIUS, upon the taking of *Megara*, asked Stilpo the philosopher what he had lost. *Nothing*, says he, *for I had all that I could call my own about me*. And yet the enemy had then made himself master of his patrimony, his children, and his country. But these he looked upon only as adventitious goods, and under the command of fortune. Now he that neither lost anything nor feared anything in a public ruin, but was safe and at peace in the middle of the flames, and in the heat of a military intemperance and fury — what violence, or provocation imaginable, can put such a man as this out of the possession of himself? Walls and castles may be mined and battered, but there is no art or engine that can subvert a steady mind. *I have made my way*, says Stilpo, *through fire and blood. What is become of my children, I know not; but these are transitory blessings, and servants that are condemned to change their masters. What was my own before, is my own still. Some have lost their estates, others*

A generous instance of a constant mind

their dear-bought mistresses, their commissions and offices; the usurers have lost their bonds and securities, but, Demetrius, *for my part, I have saved all; and do not imagine, after all this, either that* Demetrius *is a conqueror, or that* Stilpo *is overcome: it is only thy fortune has been too hard for mine. Alexander took Babylon, Scipio took Carthage; the capital was burnt*: but there is no fire or violence that can discompose a generous mind. And let us not take this character neither for a *chimera*, for all ages afford some, though not many instances of this elevated virtue. A good man does his duty, let it be never so painful, so hazardous, or never so great a loss to him; and it is not all the money, the power, and the pleasure in the world – no, not any force or necessity that can make him wicked. He considers what he is to do, not what he is to suffer, and will keep on his course, though there should be nothing but gibbets and torments in the way. And in this instance of *Stilpo*, who, when he had lost his country, his wife, his children, the town on fire over his head, himself escaping very hardly, and naked out of the flames, says, *I have saved all my goods, my justice, my courage, my temperance, and my prudence*, accounting nothing his own, or valuable, and showing how much easier it was to overcome a nation than one wise man. It is a certain mark of a brave mind not to be moved by any accidents. The upper region of the air admits neither clouds nor tempests; the thunder, storms and meteors are formed below, and this is a difference betwixt a mean and an exalted mind: the former is rude and tumultuary, the latter is modest, venerable, composed, and always quiet in its station. In brief, it is the conscience that pronounces upon the man, whether he be happy or miserable. But, though sacrilege and adultery be generally condemned, how many are there still that do not so much as blush at the one, and in truth, take a glory in the other? For nothing is more common than for great thieves to ride in triumph when the little ones are punished. *But let wickedness escape, as it may, at the bar, it never fails of doing justice upon itself, for every guilty person is his own hangman.*

✹ End of Part One ✹

*Seneca on Happiness, Virtue, and
Philosophy as the Guide to Life*
Roger L'Estrange and Keith Seddon
Published by Keith Seddon at Lulu 2009
© 2009 Keith Seddon
ISBN 978-0-9556844-7-0 (paperback)

*Typeset in Bembo Book by the editor using Microsoft Word 2007.
Proofs checked and reviewed in Portable Document Format
created using open source PDFCreator 0.9.8.*

NOTE ON THE TYPEFACE

All text is set in Bembo Book, designed by Robin Nicholas.

'Originally drawn by Monotype in 1929, the Bembo® design was inspired by the types cut by Francesco Griffo and used by Aldus Manutius in 1495 to print Cardinal Bembo's tract *De Aetna*. A beautiful design with tall ascending lowercase and elegant letterforms, Bembo has been a favourite for book setting for over 70 years. ... Considered by many to be one of Stanley Morison's finest achievements during his tenure as Typographical Advisor to the Monotype Corporation, Bembo has consistently been a bestselling typeface, both in its original hot metal form and in today's digital formats. ... This new digital version of Bembo, called Bembo Book, has been designed to be more suited to text setting in the size range from 10 point to 18 point. Based on the hot metal 10/18 point drawings, which were used to cut all sizes from 10 point to 24 point, this new face has been carefully drawn to produce similar results to those achieved from the hot metal version when letterpress printed. The project started in 2002 when a high quality UK printing house asked for a digital version of Bembo which would give a similar appearance on the page to the 13 point hot metal they were currently using. Hot metal drawings were digitised and extensive editing was carried out on the resultant outlines to ensure that design features and overall colour from the digital output remained close to that of the letterpress product. The resultant typeface is slightly narrower than existing digital versions of Bembo, it is a little more economical in use and gives excellent colour to continuous pages of text. Ascending lowercase letters are noticeably taller than capitals, giving an elegant, refined look to the text.'

(Slightly abridged from http://www.monotype.co.uk/bembo/)

www.ingramcontent.com/pod-product-compliance
Lightning Source LLC
Chambersburg PA
CBHW031415040426
42444CB00005B/573